D0519179

YESTERDAYS

YESTERDAYS

The Way We Were

1919-1939

Eric Midwinter

SOUVENIR PRESS

Copyright © 1998 by Souvenir Press Ltd

The right of Eric Midwinter to be identified as author of this
work has been asserted by him in accordance with the
Copyright, Designs and Patents Act 1988.

First published 1998 by
Souvenir Press Ltd.,
43 Great Russell Street, London WC1B 3PA

Reprinted 1999 (twice)
Reprinted 2000

All Rights Reserved. No part of this publication
may be reproduced, stored in a retrieval system,
or transmitted, in any form or by any means, electronic,
mechanical, photocopying, recording or otherwise,
without the prior permission of the Copyright owner.

ISBN 0 285 63457 7

Printed in Singapore

Every effort has been made to trace the ownership of, and where applicable
to obtain appropriate licences or permissions relating to, all copyrighted
material; in future printings, such corrections or acknowledgements (if any)
as may be necessary or desirable in consequence of our use of such material
will willingly be made.

CONTENTS

INTRODUCTION
The Between Years

Residential streets strangely empty without the close lines of parked cars, just the occasional baker's van or horse-drawn cart loaded with sacks of coal. Rooftops bare of TV aerials, giving them an odd, naked look, but most of the chimneys are smoking. Inside the houses the living-rooms are heated by coal fires and the chairs are clustered round them for warmth – no television set to form the focus of the seating arrangements. Cooking is done in the oven and on the iron range, although some gas cookers are beginning to appear.

Not, as you might think, the Britain of a century ago, but a mere sixty or seventy years. Ten million people share memories of what life was like then. Ten thousand of them were actually born in the nineteenth century, but the huge majority were born and bred between the two world wars. That is where their early memories are fixed.

Think of all the changes that have occurred since the Second World War. We have witnessed the coming of nationwide television and other electronic wizardry, notably the computer. Flying has become an everyday experience. The pill has brought well-nigh faultless birth control. The role of women has changed dramatically. We have benefited from penicillin, transplants and other medical 'miracles'. Above all, our expectations have been radically changed by the introduction of the Welfare State and the National Health Service.

The 1919-39 phase was brief but eventful, a mixture of ups and downs. This book sets out to recapture the flavour of those years, to recall through contemporary photographs how we lived and worked and enjoyed ourselves, and to show how the seeds of so much that we take for granted today were sown at that time.

Let's begin by looking at the period in its historical context. Imagine the history of the nineteenth and twentieth centuries as one long summer's day. There's an extensive morning of calm and relatively pleasant weather. There's an enjoyable evening of comparatively lovely sunshine. Unfortunately, everything is spoilt by two violent thunderstorms. The tranquil morning is the Victorian era of stability and growth. The serene evening is the post-war years of, by and large, flourishing progress.

The two storms are, of course, the world wars of 1914–18 and 1939–45. On our scale of a summer's day, they exploded about three o'clock and five o'clock in the afternoon. That left barely a couple of hours in between, two hours of what the weathermen would call unsettled and uncertain conditions.

Just twenty years separated the signing of the peace treaty in 1919 and the invasion of Poland in 1939. In historical time, it is but a twinkling of the chronological eye. One tragic war, affecting every family in the land, had just finished, but its awful effects didn't vanish overnight. Very soon there were alarms abroad and then the threat of another war. It's worth remembering that many people were involved in or affected by both World Wars.

On the world stage, Britain still had its massive Empire. Some still emigrated to the dominions – the peak year was 1923 when a quarter of a million people left these shores. Annually, on 24 May, Empire Day was celebrated, especially in the schools, but already there were one or two early stirrings of peoples seeking their independence.

Most people, however, were more worried about events in nearby Europe than in the faraway Empire. The Russian revolution of 1917 and a Bolshevik regime in Moscow provoked both suspicion and enthusiasm in Britain. The Spanish Civil War (1936–39) aroused interest among the politically active, and just over two thousand British citizens (not as many, perhaps, as one imagined) fought for the left-wing Republican cause against the eventually successful fascist coup of General Franco.

Obviously, it was the fascist regimes of Hitler's Germany and Mussolini's Italy which were soon giving rise to most direct anxiety, even if our own example of that – Oswald Mosley's Blackshirts, formed in 1932 – was never a real threat. We appeared to be heading straight from one war to the next. At home, both people and politicians were, on the whole, very inward-looking. Perhaps most people are like this most of the time, but the mood was peculiarly insular

then. There was none of the grandeur and sweep of other eras before and since. The most typical leader of the age was Stanley Baldwin, the Conservative prime minister in 1923, 1924–29 and 1935–37. His avuncular 'You Can Trust Me' image and famous policy of 'Safety First' fitted the times admirably. About the only colourful interlude was the Abdication Crisis of 1936, when Edward VIII yielded up the throne to his brother, George VI, over his wish to marry the American divorcee, Mrs Simpson. Even this was a rather transient, local affair, soon over and leaving almost everyone strangely unaffected. The 1937 Coronation, however, provided a moment of national celebration.

The Great Depression dominated economic life. There was untold unemployment and poverty, at its most rampant around 1929–33, when as many as four million were out of work. Counting in their families, this meant that seven million – a sixth of the nation – were living on the meagre dole. There were still a million unemployed as late as 1940.

The dole began at fifteen shillings (75p) a week for a male worker, with extras for dependants, at a time when the average manual wage was just under three pounds a week. But the dole was means-tested after what was the statutory period of fifteen weeks' payment, and, in any case, poorly paid workers not in the National Insurance scheme had to resort to the poor law for support. Tales of pawned wedding rings abound in the folk-memories of districts, such as Jarrow, where unemployment stood as high as 66 per cent over several years. The Jarrow March of the unemployed to London became a symbol of that suffering which left a lasting scar on so many lives.

Before that there had been the General Strike of May 1926, when the country seemed paralysed and on the verge of rebellion, but which, apart from the embattled miners, fizzled out like a damp squib. Such flare-ups were rare and extinguished quickly. Generally speaking, it was a time of quiet despondency rather than of the much more violent reaction of the slump in the USA.

People's memories of the period differ according to where they were living then. The depression hit harshly at the old heavy industrial areas like Clydeside, Tyneside, the South Welsh mining valleys and the textile districts of Lancashire and the West Riding of Yorkshire. It was much less damaging in the light industrial areas of the Midlands and the Home Counties.

To the despair of historians anxious to hear the word of contemporary witnesses, most older people have little or no memory of the great events, unless they were among the comparatively small minority directly involved in them. What they do recall is the everyday fabric of life, what they ate and who came to the door and what was on the wireless.

Nearly everyone remembers how the oil and gas lamps were ousted and electricity came to many households. The supply of electricity – the National Grid was established during this time – and the resulting output of electrical goods both doubled during the 1930s. These were not principally as yet the larger items. The Americans bought more refrigerators than the British in the proportion of twenty to one at this time. It was items like light bulbs and reading lamps that were purchased – and also vacuum cleaners. The annual production of vacuum cleaners sprang astronomically from 38,000 in 1930 to 410,000 in 1935.

Despite the depression, industrial output per head actually rose by a third between 1924 and 1937. This remains one of the greatest increases ever recorded. There was an emphatic growth in the number of firms making such things as safety razors, tinned vegetables, cheap cosmetics, toothpaste, artificial textiles, fountain pens and bicycles.

If it was a time of low wages, it was also a time of low costs and prices. Only the very poor and the permanently unemployed were prevented from enjoying real improvements in their standard of living.

* * *

As regards foodstuffs, the most important change between the wars was the emergence of large-scale concerns with heavily branded products, of which Tate & Lyle's almost complete monopoly of the sugar-refining trade is a good example. Although 80,000 grocers, 40,000 butchers, 30,000 bakers and 30,000 greengrocers still existed as single-shop owners, they were increasingly retailing well-advertised, branded products rather than blending their own tea or curing their own bacon.

The branded goods brought the convenience of 'table-readiness' to the housewife. The complexities of making jellies, blancmanges and custards were eased by the sale of prepared packets, while, from the pre-1914 simplicity of 'plain' and 'milk', arose a bewildering variety of Cadbury and Rowntree chocolates in 2d (1p) bars and sixpenny (2.5p) boxes.

The range of canned goods offered by Heinz and Crosse & Blackwell also expanded enormously from the very few tins on offer before 1914. Sunday tea might well have consisted of tinned salmon, followed by tinned pineapple chunks or peaches. Even potatoes – and three-quarters of all British main meals around 1936 included potatoes – were now processed. By 1938 over a million packets of crisps, notably Smith's with the elusive blue paper twist of salt, were being sold annually.

Porridge, the near-universal middle-class breakfast dish, could now be prepared in two minutes, courtesy of the Quick Quaker Oats recipe, but even so, it found a rival in the new cereals coming on to the market. Processed breakfast cereals had their origins in American health food notions. For example, J.H. Kellogg was a physician with a sanatorium, and his brother, W.K. Kellogg, used the cereal grain foods eaten there as the base of his cornflake empire. 'Force' and 'Grape-nuts' were the early products, soon followed by cornflakes and a spread of 'puffed' grains of wheat, barley and rice.

Many will recall from those days the beginnings of colourful modern advertising. There was the cheerful appeal of Sunny Jim and his breakfast cereals and many other adverts of this same health-conscious nature were current. 'Don't get tired — Drink Bovril' was one such example; the benefits of Horlick's malted milk for 'night starvation' another. Both the 'Eat More Fruit' and 'Drink More Milk' advertisements scored great successes. More seriously, the government had a major triumph with its diphtheria immunisation campaign. There were also the tuneful blandishments of the Ovaltinies or the Cocoacubs, increasingly brought to our notice by Radio Luxembourg, a commercial antidote to the somewhat stuffy image of the BBC and, if still small in impact, a portent of the media advertising of the post-war world.

Above all, these years saw the spread of the motor car. It was nowhere near as dominant as it would be in the post-1945 years, but, looking back, we can see what led to today's over-packed, car-jammed roads.

It was during this time that the motor car gradually replaced the domestic servant as the crucial middle-class status symbol. By 1931 only five per cent of households had servants, whereas in Victorian times even homes with moderate incomes had had a servant or two. Most older people are likely to recall some of their own relations having been servants or having employed servants. They'll also no doubt remember their first ride in a car.

For the number of motor vehicles shot from about a million just after the Great War to some four million by the outbreak of the next war. This included an increase in private cars from 200,000 in 1921 to nearly two million in 1939. Sadly, it also meant the scourge of road deaths – 7,342 were killed in 1934, compared with 3,598 in 1996 when 38 million vehicles were registered. This carnage led to the introduction of driving tests, if only for new drivers, and of a 30 miles per hour speed limit. The Belisha Beacon, still used for zebra crossings, was named after the then Minister of Transport, Leslie Hore-Belisha, as part of his road safety campaign.

Public transport had been revolutionised in the nineteenth century by the railways. Now it was the turn of the bus, virtually unknown outside London and a few large cities before 1914. Now buses and trolley buses began to replace trams in the towns and then, especially in country areas, buses began to challenge the train.

Together the car and the bus actually changed the shape of towns. Previously they had been very compact, with the railway station at the hub and tramcars to carry passengers fairly short distances, usually to and from the station or the town centre. Buses, cars, vans and lorries were much more flexible. What became known as 'ribbon' housing development was now possible. Instead of cramped sets of terraced streets, houses could be built in long straggling lines.

Towns became more spread out and scattered as new housing estates were constructed out of town. Welwyn Garden City, started in 1920, and second to Letchworth Garden City (1903), forms a valuable, if specialised, illustration. Not only did it provide pleasant, well-appointed housing with a rural belt, it also included light manufacturing companies like printing, foodstuffs and radios. Although there were to be only two 'garden cities' in Britain, they foreshadowed the great post-war outcrop of 'new towns' such as Hemel Hempstead and Harlow.

Another way in which the 1920s and '30s formed a bridge from one great age to another, therefore, was in housing. As with car usage, this was a movement which was to grow massively after 1945.

Between the wars three million new private houses and one million council houses were constructed – and there had been only 24,000 council houses in 1914. By 1939, as many as two-fifths of Britain's ten million homes had been built since 1914. In 1914 90 per cent of households were privately rented; today the figure is less than ten per cent. The inter-war years saw the start of that shift.

The ambitious lower middle class aspired to own a semi-detached private home. The respectable working class aspired to rent a new council house. Costs were not exorbitant. A weekly mortgage repayment might be as low as 8s (40p), not much more than the average weekly council house rental of 6s or 7s (30/35p). To put that in perspective, 60 per cent of people in the 1930s had a weekly income of between £2 10s and £5, with a further 20 per cent earning between £5 and £10. In other words, decent housing was within the scope of the extending ranks of tradesmen and office workers.

Many of these houses were furnished by hire-purchase. The 'never-never' enabled families to fill their homes with furniture and gadgets. A typical bedroom suite cost about £28 and blankets might be £1 3s 6d (£1.17p) a pair. There would be a little garden, and houses boasted a hall or lobby, a kitchen or living-room, and the inevitable 'front room', only used on special occasions.

What has been called 'the religion of home-improvement' made many converts. There was lots of painting and decorating and putting up of shelves, a foretaste of the present-day mania for DIY. Despite the arrival of electric light, there was little central heating, indeed, little heating at all apart from the open coal fire in the room in main use. As the historian, A.J.P. Taylor, pertinently remarked, 'chilblains remained a unique English malady'.

Most people during this period were still taking holidays on home soil. The boarding houses of the famous seaside resorts remained the main beneficiaries, with the caravan and the youth hostel – the first one was opened in 1930 – also now playing a part. Different regions favoured different stretches of the coastline. Londoners flocked to Margate and Brighton; Yorkshire people chose Scarborough and Skegness; Midlanders visited North Wales, Bournemouth and Torquay; Lancastrians trooped in their thousands to Southport, Morecambe and,

inevitably, Blackpool. The Blackpool boarding house normally charged twenty-eight shillings (£1.40) a week for a double bed and the visitors would 'buy in' food which the landlady cooked.

Air travel and foreign holidays were mainly the province of the rich. The half-crown (12.5p) flip round the local aerodrome or the rather self-conscious ship and train visit to the Swiss Alps were just hints of the vast airborne exodus of post-war Britons to the Costa Brava and beyond.

A minority of people, particularly the young well-to-do, adopted more frenetic modes of behaviour, somewhat removed from the buckets and spades of Cleethorpes or Southend. Some of these were imported from America and included dances, clothes and music of a slightly bizarre kind. Those endearing images of hoppity Charlestons and Black Bottoms, of slim-line, abbreviated dresses surmounted by frizzled, shingled hair-dos, form, even today, the cultural short-hand for the era.

Whether it was the jazz of Louis Armstrong or the melodies of Irving Berlin, the American place in popular music of the time was assured. However, there were also British musicians in profusion – the Performing Rights Society had over 40,000 composers on its books in the 1920s. The dance band – Debroy Somers, Joe Loss, Geraldo, Henry Hall, Jack Hylton – was a well-entrenched institution, curiously cross-class. Jack Payne's Orchestra played at the Cecil Hotel, London, for the rich and famous, but, as Director of the BBC Dance Orchestra, he led an enlarged version of his hotel band in bringing the same music to all classes via the wireless. Similarly, Henry Hall conducted the dance band at Manchester's fashionable Midland Hotel prior to his enormous impact as a broadcaster. Joe Loss was in demand as a society band-leader, but for years holiday-makers enjoyed dancing to his rhythms at the Villa Marina in Douglas, Isle of Man.

For the more sedate dancing of the waltz or the slow fox-trot, the band leader Bert Ambrose would instruct his orchestra never to play so loudly that they could not hear the swish of the frocks on the dance-floor. It was in this period that the allure of the commercial dance hall reached its zenith, and many a courtship ripened under the slowly swirling lights of a Mecca or Ritz ballroom.

One of the most popular forms of entertainment was 'going to the pictures', often with Shirley Temple, Rudolph Valentino or the cowboy star, Tom Mix, on the bill. The cinema epitomises entertainment for the 1920s and '30s. On the one hand, it was not 'live', thereby pointing forward to the technological entertainment of today, such as videos and CD players. On the other hand, it was an act of getting together. Leisure in those days was frequently about 'going out', often with the family and often in big crowds.

The cinema inherited this idea of family outings from the theatre, which itself had only become respectable, with the aid of Gilbert and Sullivan, in the fifty years leading up to 1914. Throughout this period the popular theatre tried to hold its own. The old music hall had gone, to be replaced with 'variety', with stars like Gracie Fields, Max Miller and Anne Ziegler and Webster Booth topping the bills. The Christmas pantomime and the seaside summer concert party were other outlets for live entertainment.

Film-going, although frowned upon by some, was regarded by most as quite innocent, and people flocked to their local Regal or Embassy. With Charlie Chaplin at the helm, the cinema had, of course, already made its mark, but it was the advent in 1927 of the 'talkies' which transformed its public appeal. By 1939 the cinema was near to the pinnacle it enjoyed in the following decade. Britain had some 5,000 cinemas by the outbreak of the Second World War.

Two-fifths of the population visited their cinema once a week and a quarter twice a week. The old commissionaire's cry to those queuing of 'one and nines on the right; half a crown round the corner', that is 8p or 12.5p, gives some idea of the higher prices. Tickets for children's Saturday matinées,

maybe to watch Flash Gordon or Buck Jones serials, were as low as 4d (2p) and the 'penny-crush' in the local 'flea-pit' or 'bug-hut' was by no means unknown.

Take one Saturday night at random – 25 April, 1931, in Liverpool. While Sophie Tucker kept alive the variety tradition at the Empire Theatre, there was a choice of nine films in the city centre: from Spencer Tracy in 'Up the River' to Zane Grey's cowboy epic, 'The Light of the Western Stars'. Of course, all the cinemas would be closed on the following day, Sunday.

Another popular form of collective, but live, entertainment was sport. The Football League teams, like Arsenal, Aston Villa, Newcastle United and Huddersfield Town, all attracted huge 'gates', and in 1923 a vastly overcrowded Wembley staged its first FA Cup Final, Bolton Wanderers beating West Ham United. Test and county cricket was still very popular. It was the era of all-conquering Yorkshire in the County Championship and of the prodigious Australian batsman, Don Bradman, on the international scene.

By contrast, the introduction of the 'wireless' was as influential in the other direction: radio kept people at home. In 1926 the British Broadcasting Corporation was founded as a public body by royal charter. By the early 1930s some five million wireless licences were held and by the beginning of the war, awaiting radio's finest hour, nine out of every ten households had a wireless.

The BBC gradually built a middle-of-the-road audience across all the nation's classes and regions. With the dour and puritanical John Reith in charge, it offered the middle-brow diet of music, drama, current affairs and religious worship which he felt was best for the listeners. More slowly, light entertainment was added.

Many men and women, now over 65, are able to quote catch-phrases and sayings of their childhood's 'wireless' characters, such as Larry the Lamb or Ernest the Policeman from 'Toytown', a series also popular during and after the Second World War. Of older vintage were radio's first comic characters: Helen Millais as 'Our Lizzie'; the John Henry and Blossom couple, with the first broadcast catch-phrase, 'John Henry, Come on', and Mabel Constanduros in her 'Mrs Buggins' role. Later there were Arthur Askey and Richard 'Stinker' Murdoch on 'Bandwagon', 'In Town Tonight', the 'Kentucky Minstrels', and Reginald Foort and Sandy Macpherson at the BBC theatre organ.

In the years after the war, television, in terms of popularity, would successfully challenge both cinema and radio. Like the cinema, it provided pictures. Like the radio, it was for home enjoyment. The cinema looked back more to the days of collective leisure, while the wireless gazed ahead to that privacy of leisure in the home so prominent after 1950. Neither radio nor cinema would ever again be quite so influential as they were in the inter-war and war years.

The gramophone too came into its own at this time. It resembled the radio in that it encouraged the enjoyment of music at home, whereas hitherto people had had to go to the concert hall or sit round the bandstand. At the same time, it discouraged personal playing. The radio and gramophone began to replace the piano in the parlours of the land. The gramophone became especially popular after 1926 when electrical replaced acoustic recording. The heavy black 78rpm records, with best-sellers like George Formby, Sandy Powell, Peter Dawson, Gracie Fields, Dame Clara Butt and Ernest Lush the boy soprano, were the forerunners of today's compact discs.

Even gambling was already possible at home. Although betting, especially on horses and greyhounds, remained a largely male-dominated activity, the chequered Littlewoods pools form was typically completed at home, by women as well as men. It was a stepping-stone towards the televised lottery, with one's ticket electronically registered.

During this period an Englishman's home gradually became both his castle and his sanctuary. One pleasing result was the reduction in convictions for drunkenness, from 189,000 in 1913 to 53,000 in 1930. Tea-drinking continued to flourish. In the 1840s the average annual consumption of tea had been 1.6lbs per individual. By the 1930s it was close on 7lbs.

Yet there remained much of the past. There were, for instance, still a lot of horses around, not only in the countryside but in the towns, particularly carrying coal and other heavy goods from the railways sidings. It is this kind of dichotomy that makes the period such a confusion of past and future things. There were horses to remind us of the past, and aeroplanes and gramophones to hint at what the future would bring. The 1920s and '30s were the hinge years, the between years, of modern British social history.

There remained wide differences in the way people lived and behaved. There were still wealthy landowners and hard-working farmers in the countryside and also many very poorly paid farm labourers – in 1936 a third of the children of all farm-workers were ill-fed and under-nourished. Nor had the grimy poverty of the industrial towns vanished – rickets and tuberculosis and other complaints, in part the consequence of poor housing and unhealthy diet, were still rife. The upper classes maintained high standards of luxury living. London nightclubs, like the 'Kit-Kat', the 'Manhattan' and the 'Silver Slipper', offered opulent wining and dining to a wealthy and well-connected clientele. Cruising on the luxury liner *Queen Mary*, or wintering in the South of France, was an affluent upper crust indulging in a resplendent life-style.

But somewhere within this varied pattern a new Britain was emerging. Unshaped and unprogrammed, it was the semi-detached life of the suburb, and it was fast becoming the ambition of the vast majority to live that kind of life.

IN THE STREET

Men came pouring back from France at the end of the 1914-18 war and Britain tried to settle to a peaceful routine. Many roads were bedecked with 'Welcome Home' flags and there were plenty of street parties – indeed for many people the street was the centre for social life at this time. It therefore seems the ideal place to start our walk down Memory Lane.

Funnily enough, it's what you wouldn't have seen then that is most significant. Glance down a residential road or high street now and you will see lines of cars, sometimes two and three to a house. Glance down the same street at roof-level and you will see the metal sculptures of TV aerials and, increasingly, satellite dishes, above every building.

Then there was more of an emptiness. One or two motor vehicles were creeping in, but the rooftops were clear, excepting, of course, for the smoke coming from every chimney. When vehicles did appear in residential areas they often carried doorstep deliveries. Some were still horse-drawn, while some shops relied on the unsteady progress of an errand-boy on an unwieldy bike. Groceries, greengroceries, meat, bread, stone bottles of dandelion and burdock – they could all be ordered and delivered or simply purchased at the door.

However, you would have seen more children playing in the streets. There was no danger from traffic and no telly to keep them indoors. Those children, today's pensioners, will tell you of street-games, all solemnly played according to iron-cast rules, with the lamp-post performing the duty, for instance, of goal-post in the winter and wicket in the summer. It also served as a skipping-rope turner or as the rallying-point for innumerable brands of 'ticky'.

The houses themselves were changing. Now there were council houses and suburban 'semis'. It was everyone's ambition to rent or own a two- or three-bedroomed semi-detached house, or maybe a bungalow, with an emphasis on 'all mod cons'.

Many more houses now had an indoor lavatory, and such sophistication encouraged the purchase of proper toilet rolls, although the prudent householder still preferred carefully scissored squares of newspaper. Some may recollect the anguish of trying, while comfortably seated, to read some fascinating article from these 'squares', only to find that the crucial portion had already been utilised!

A nice ordinary house of this type became the average household. This is the time when the model family of mother, father, son and daughter became the stock characters of school reading books and retail advertising. The Ovaltinies were in the ascendant.

Leys Avenue, Letchworth, a typical high street soon after World War I. It is the absence of cars on a busy shopping day which makes it so different from today. There are just a couple of cars, square and solid in shape, but there are plenty of bikes and plenty of space for the pedestrians. Another interesting point is the mix of big 'shop' names – Woolworth's, Home and Colonial Stores – with small, probably one-family businesses, like the furnishings shop on the left.

Photo: Mary Evans/Town and Country Planning

Spath Lane, Handforth, Cheshire, exactly the sort of neat little bungalow, almost chalet-like, being sought by the rising number of owner-occupiers at this time. It was one of the first to be built after the First World War and, with 'all mod cons', detached, and set in its own little garden, it was quite luxurious. The tall chimney to the right reminds us that solid fuel would still be required for heating and hot water.

Photo: Documentary Photography Archive

This new block of flats, built in the 1930s, illustrates another answer to the search for homes. Outside of London and bigger cities, flat-life was scarcely known before World War I. Gaunt and a trifle daunting, they foreshadow the even higher, and often socially disastrous, flats constructed after World War II. The streets are still almost empty of cars, but a solitary telephone wire and three wireless 'masts' show that progress is on the move.

Photo: Mary Evans/Margaret Monck

A street in a working class area in 1930, with not a TV aerial or satellite dish in sight, and only a very occasional lamp-post. There is not one car to be seen. Yet it's a crowded scene, with lots of children at play, and plenty of parents, chiefly mothers, keeping a watchful eye. We would be surprised to find a street anywhere today with upward of thirty children out and about and so many front doors open.

Photo: Mary Evans Picture Library

A main road in Pinner, Middlesex, in 1923. The cyclist and friend chat in the middle of the main road; the horse has a tranquil drink at the trough; even the man with the brush pauses for a natter. This is a very peaceful picture near the Queen's Head Hotel, whose sign informs us that we are only thirteen miles from busy London. Seventy years on and it's a scene of roaring traffic and hubbub.

Photo: Mary Evans Picture Library

A Metropolitan Police box from the 1920s. Street furniture is always indicative of how life is changing. Policemen had formerly communicated with one another by the use of their whistles; now the telephone was being frequently used to report in or ask for assistance. It wasn't yet the mobile phones and personal radio contact of the modern day, but it was a step in that direction.

Photo: © Barnaby's Picture Library

A K3 telephone kiosk at Great Yarmouth, 1936: the familiar sight of the GPO telephone kiosk, by now appearing in great numbers at appropriate points. Very few people could afford or felt the need for a private phone, so that the public service was in huge demand. This couple are sending a telegram by phone, and the telegram was another technical device being increasingly used by the public.

Photo: By courtesy of BT Archives

Young James Fawcett minds his father's cart in Third Street, Trafford Park, Stretford in the 1930s. Most houses had either a circular man-hole or a small door in the wall leading to the coal-cellar where, each week, the likes of Mr Fawcett would deliver several lumpy hundredweight sacks of coal. Most coalmen wore metal-thonged leather jackets for protection. The horse found one of its last urban roles in the haulage of coal carts.

Photo: Documentary Photography Archive

A baker's van in Ripley, Derbyshire. Among the commonest motor vehicles during this period were those bringing goods to the house. Two 'breadmen', as they were called, pose by the side of their 'bread van' which brought loaves, cobs, muffins and cakes to the housewives' doors. Grocers and greengrocers provided other examples of doorstep deliveries which, as a daily occurrence, have all but disappeared, except for the milkman.

Photo: Derbyshire Libraries and Heritage Department

A London flower-seller in the 1930s, pictured against the background of 'the roar of London's traffic' (as the announcer used to say on the BBC's 'In Town Tonight' programme) with buses and a taxi making up a typically busy scene. The introduction to 'In Town Tonight' also included a street-cry of 'violets, sweet violets', and flower-vending has survived as one of very few examples of street-trading in the big cities.

Photo: © Barnaby's Picture Library

AT HOME

Let's take a look inside the average house of the pre-war years. Think of how we arrange the furniture now. Right away you'll spot two distinct differences, compared with the normal household shape sixty or seventy years ago.

First of all, the huge majority of homes were still heated by coal fires. Although some had gas stoves, coal fires also provided for much of the cooking. As well as that, coal fires were used for the warming of flat irons for pressing purposes and, very frequently, for hot water. Many will remember the complexities of pushing in or pulling out the 'damper' which controlled the mysteries of heating the water.

Usually the sole fire was in the living-room and the family tended to arrange themselves around it, clustering ever closer as winter drew draughtily nigh. The inclination was to gather in the one relatively warm room. Today, courtesy of central heating, both residents and chairs may be distributed more widely – which brings us to the second chief difference.

By the 1930s it was usual to have a wireless in any self-respecting home. You didn't need to stare straight at it. You could sit on top of the fire and listen to Debroy Somers and the Savoy Orpheans with the wireless tucked away in the corner. Or you could do the same with the increasingly popular gramophone. These two features have created opposites. In yesterday's living-room the seating surrounded the fire; in today's living-room it encircles the television.

You just couldn't ignore the importance of that solitary fire in the living-room. For a start, coal-fired heating involved major storage. Forty million tons of coal were annually sold on the domestic market, and householders had to put it somewhere. The coal-shed or coal-cellar was a feature now long gone. Every week the coal cart would come clattering round and the coalman would tipple hundredweight bags of coal into your coal-cellar. Heat, or the lack of it, even affected going to bed. Ask members of the older generation about the pre-war bedroom and they'll groan about the problems of keeping warm. They might have used a hot-water bottle, with water heated on the kitchen fire. They might have sought the perilous aid of a sharp-edged fire-brick, warmed in the kitchen oven, wrapped in an old woolly, and apt to do the restless sleeper's legs a terrible mischief at dead of night. One of the clearest and most oft-repeated memories from those times is of rising on a cold and frosty morning and 'putting my bare feet on the lino'.

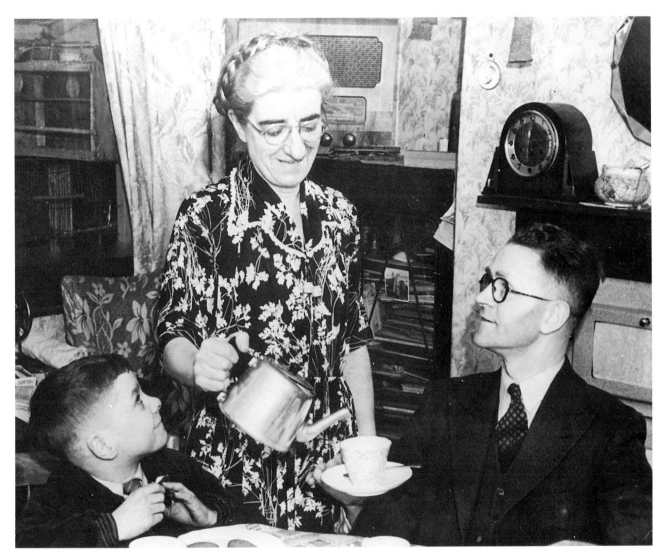

The Ross family enjoy a placid, characteristically British tea-time in Manchester in the 1930s. The sense of calm and security is very pronounced, as, with all three quite formally dressed, they settle down for afternoon tea. The wireless is behind them, and one would like to think that the voice of Uncle Mac on 'Children's Hour' is a further soothing influence. Today they would be more likely to be sitting facing the television with a cup of tea in their lap.

Photo: Documentary Photography Archive

Mr and Mrs Blackshaw of Darwen in a time-flash self-portrait. They read quietly around the glowing coal fire in another typical living-room portrayal. You had to keep close to the fire for warmth, and this dictated the lay-out of living-room furniture. The fire-place is modern, indicating that the Blackshaws had a separate kitchen for cooking. Note again how dress is highly respectable, despite this being a relaxed time of the day. Mr Blackshaw is wearing slippers, but his collar and tie are intact.

Photo: Documentary Photography Archive

Anne Roberts and Pamela Farley, pictured in a rather well appointed living-room in 1938, about to play a heavyweight 78rpm record on one of the old-style wind-up gramophones which grew increasingly popular at this time. Sometimes the record slowed, the sound became slurred and you had to rush to rewind the gramophone. Gramophones were mobile: you might have heard one at a picnic or being used at a local church hall 'social' for dancing.

Photo: Hulton Getty

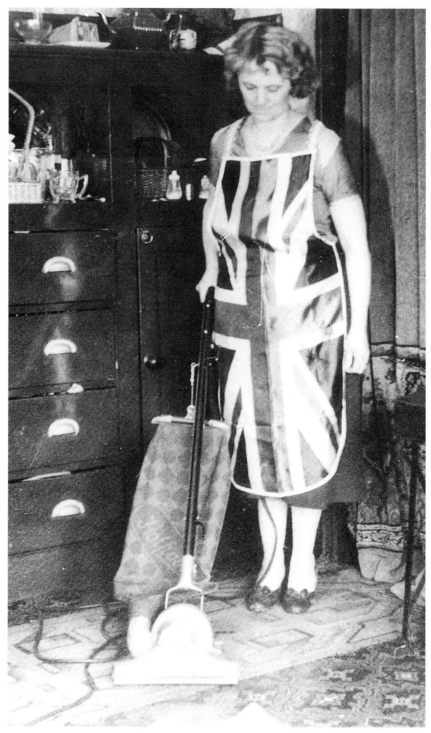

Mrs Whitham of Stretford proudly uses her Hotpoint vacuum cleaner, with her 1937 Coronation apron giving away the date of the photograph. The vacuum cleaner was the symbol of the new technological approach to housework. Not every household had one, partly because of the expense, partly, of course, because you had to have electricity. The manual Ewbank carpet sweeper was much used and at a time when fitted carpets were rare, many carpets and rugs were slung over the washing line and subjected to a severe thumping with a special 'carpet beater'.

Photo: Documentary Photography Archive

A typical 1930s kitchen. It is much improved on a 1900s kitchen, with its pull-down work surface as part of fitted cupboards, but it is still rather undeveloped by modern standards. Note the flat irons heating up on the coal-fuelled stove, the nearby coal scuttle and the carton of Vim, for cleaning purposes, on the shelf, alongside the aluminium pans. It looks as if cakes are being made, but there is no sign of an automatic mixer.

Photo: © Barnaby's Picture Library

Mrs Witham of Stretford again, still wearing her Coronation apron, but this time busy at her gas stove. By the 1930s gas stoves were fast replacing the coal-fired range and oven – which had often been in the main living-room – as the main cooking mode, but central heating remained rare. The heavy lidless pans, boiling away merrily, remind us both of the condensation in kitchens then and also of the tendency to over-cook vegetables and much else.

Photo: Documentary Photography Archive

A Newcastle upon Tyne bedroom in 1924. Tastefully decorated, curtained and furnished, this bedroom was used by the Philipson's company in their 'Electricity in the Home' exhibition. The stylish overhead and dressing-table lamps illustrate the growing use of electricity for domestic purposes in the post-1919 years. This was mainly for lighting and houses might have been fully lit by electricity and have no wall plugs. Then the use of electric fires, radios, vacuum cleaners and so on gradually developed.

Photo: Newcastle Libraries and Information Service

A 1930s bathroom, rather splendid and tiled throughout. Nothing better illustrates the comforts sought by the inter-war householder than the building of homes with indoor bathrooms and lavatories. This is a rather modish example, and many bathrooms in older houses were rather more primitive, perhaps converted from a small bedroom. They also tended to be either rather chilly or full of steam.

Photo: © Barnaby's Picture Library

ON THE MOVE

How did people move around in the 1920s and '30s to get to the shops or to school and work? Nowadays the average European's daily travel is an amazing 32 kilometres. That's the result of fleets of aircraft and unending stretches of motor-way, and it is eight times the average daily travel for the period 1919-39. Even so, compared to the slower pre-1914 years, people were definitely much more on the move.

Workers and housewives required more public transport. With work, shops, schools and leisure facilities often some distance away from the home, walking to such places became much rarer than in the pre-1914 era.

The transport that answered the call was a mix of the old and the new. Horses still played their noble part. From their peak of 3,250,000 at the turn of the century, there were still approaching 3,000,000 in the 1920s. Half of them were in the towns, where their steaming manure was much sought after by the new breed of urban gardener. Many of them were used by the railways, that glorious crown of Victorian industrial progress. There was no further major development of rail, but trains, some of them now electrified, were still widely used.

Looking more to the future, the motor car was making substantial progress, although not yet to the astronomical degree of the post-1945 years. Between the wars the car passed from being the plaything of the rich to becoming the day-by-day transport of the middle class. There was a ten-fold expansion in private car owner-ship, so that cars were now familiar sights. Indeed, a popular theory of the time was that wanting a car was the cause of declining birth-rates: 'the nursery gave place to the garage'. Perhaps it was fitting that the *Baby* Austin, a seven horse-power vehicle first marketed in 1922, led the field.

The true symbol of inter-war years travel was, however, the motor bus. It was more flexible than either the train or the tram. The tram became less prominent from the mid-1920s and the last horse-drawn buses deserted London's streets in 1914. The bus, scarcely known outside London before World War I, was suddenly all the rage. Members of the current older generation, whether town or country folk, will tell you how the bus freed up both economic and social life. By 1932 it was carrying more passengers than the train.

Trolley buses at Devon Bank, Newcastle upon Tyne, 1935. Trolley buses were a hybrid of tram and bus, more manoeuvrable than the former, but confined, of course, to their overhead electric wires, and only found in larger towns. There they survived until well after the Second World War, the sparks flashing above them on the wires. They are an excellent example of the early application of electricity to public transport.

Photo: Newcastle Libraries and Information Service

Blackfriars Bridge, May 1936. The 1919-39 era was the heyday of the bus; and here is London's Blackfriars Bridge packed solid with buses and trams, all of them replete with advertisments. The mixture is fascinating. As well as the long lines of trams and the more flexible buses, there are commercial vehicles of all descriptions, taxi-cabs, an ambulance, and still quite a proportion of horse-drawn vehicles.

Photo: Mary Evans Picture Library

The Clarion Cycling Club on the Isle of Man, 1925. Hiking and biking were important escapes, especially for townsfolk, and the bicycle was an inexpensive and sociable form of transport. Householders near football grounds, for instance, used their back-yards to 'mind' fans' bikes for a penny or twopence a time. The bike was used for travelling to and from work, for deliveries of many kinds, as well as for leisure, as in this case where two young women and a schoolboy have managed to penetrate what was often an adult male preserve.

Photo: Documentary Photography Archive

Paddington Station between the wars: plenty of trains, good old solid Great Western Railway stock, and, compared with today, plenty of porters to help with luggage. In the foreground of platform one there are reminders that rail was the chief, if not the sole, long distance carrier of newspapers, post and other such freight. 'Dining and Tea Room' seems quaint where now a range of quickly-vended food and drink is on offer, but overall there is also something timeless about a railway terminus.   *Photo: Donald McLeish/Popperfoto* (Inset) **An old-style wheel-tapper**, with his sounding hammer, ensures that the goods carriages are in proper order.   *Photo: Popperfoto*

A young mother waits at Southampton Railway (now Southampton Harbour) Terminus in 1933. That good old solid pram was useful for carrying the shopping and other things as well as baby, especially in a time when cars were still uncommon. The pram was has largely given way now to collapsible buggies and papoose-type harnesses. The W.H Smith bookstall behind offers tantalising glimpses of newspaper and magazine posters with their long-forgotten news items.

Photo: Courtesy of W. H. Smith

Road-building near Newcastle upon Tyne, 1924. With increased mobility and many more motor vehicles, lots of roads were constructed and many others modernised. Road-builders and road-menders were a frequent sight, and, compared with today, it was a very laborious business. It's buckets and barrels and shovels to the fore, although this roadway does have metal strengtheners, rather than just the more straightforward tar macadam. And there are no prizes for guessing which is the foreman.

Photo: Newcastle Libraries and Information Service

Shanklin, Isle of Wight, 1924. Horses were still much in vogue, in the country, as in this delightful shot of a haycart being pulled between low-slung thatched roofs. Despite the advance of the motor vehicle, horses were still retained for certain tasks in the towns … but times were changing …

Photo: Mary Evans Picture Library

Croydon Airport, London 1935. This was one of London's key pre-war airports, and here a group of intrepid passengers are boarding for a Lufthansa flight to Germany. The inter-war years saw the early beginnings of regular civil aviation, but one did not see an aeroplane often. For many years to come, a cricket match would halt if a plane flew over – it would be difficult to finish a match under such conditions now.

Photo: Hulton Getty

AT THE SHOPS

Whether you walked or caught a bus, you had to do your shopping. Many of today's senior citizens will recall rows of specialist shops where now the supermarket holds universal sway. It has been said that 'all England became suburban' in the years between the wars. Half the population now lived in towns with more than 50,000 inhabitants; 80 per cent lived in urban areas. The general store of the old-style farming or industrial village yielded to the typical range of shops in the typical high street in the typical town.

The sort of shops which are so clearly remembered were both family businesses and chain-stores. There were the local butchers, bakers, greengrocers, ironmongers, cobblers and, in traditional straw caddies, fishmongers. But, next to them, the high streets of quite small townships might boast a Boot's, an American-style Woolworth's (then 'the threepenny and sixpenny store') a W.H. Smith's, a Montague Burton's ('the fifty shilling tailors' – that is, a suit for £2.50 in new currency) and a Freeman, Hardy and Willis.

The national takings of the retail business were, by the 1930s, almost exactly split in half between the 700,000 small-scale shopkeepers and these chains and multiples, plus the long-standing co-operative stores, which continued to be very popular.

Housewives went to the shops much more frequently than people do now when, with a car, a supermarket and a fridge-freezer, many manage a weekly 'shop'. It was often then a daily, sometimes a twice-daily, task. You had to carry sufficient for that day's meals only, otherwise many food-stuffs would perish for lack of proper storage. Older people frequently comment on the pre-packaging and open display of today. Sixty years ago the shopper stood at the counter and slowly proceeded through a series of weighings out and baggings up. The cheese would be cut and the butter slapped and shaped, the bacon sliced, the biscuits weighed, the eggs counted . . .

Let us seize on one tiny, poignant emblem of consumer activity, often referred to now by those with long memories. It is the much frowned-upon cigarette. Soldiers in the trenches and women on war-work during the 1914-18 war had adopted the cigarette. Socially permitted in public places like trains (where it was the non-smoking oddballs who had to seek out the labelled compartment) and cinemas (where one watched the latest Ronald Colman through a bluish haze), the cigarette became universal, driving the expensive cigar and the pipe to the margins. Yes, it was definitely the age of the Woodbine.

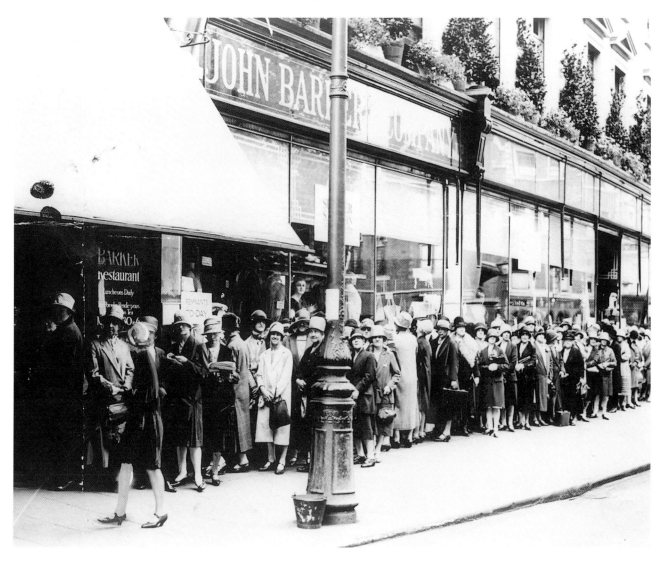

John Barker's sale, Kensington High Street, London 1928. Some things haven't changed: an extremely female-dominated throng awaits the opening of the sales – it's 'remnants today' – just as they might nowadays. The department store, not only in the cities, but in relatively small towns, was now an important feature of the high street. One thing that has changed is the fashions, in particular the wearing of hats. There isn't one hatless woman in this picture.

Photo: Mary Evans Picture Library

Fenwick's Department Store, Newcastle upon Tyne, in the early 1930s. Boxes of jams are being delivered by motor lorry, but there is also the contrast of a horse-drawn milk-float, laden with churns, outside the store. Department stores reigned supreme in the high street, with many of them in local family hands and all dealing with a huge array of items. Architecturally the department store sought to be, as it is here, an imposing edifice, welcoming but grand, not unlike the best hotels of the period.

Photo: Newcastle Libraries and Information Service

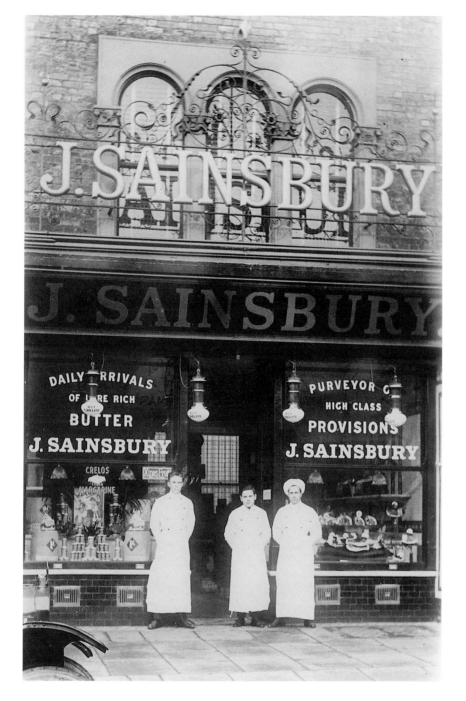

J. Sainsbury, about 1920. The grocery chain store was a late Victorian phenomenon, notably, as in the case of Thomas Lipton, based on tea sales. Betwen the wars Sainsbury's, and their rivals International Tea and the Lever Brothers/Unilever group (Home and Colonial, Lipton's, Meadow Dairies, Mac Fisheries) came to dominate the grocery business in many towns. As visible in this picture, preserves, cold meats and fats, such as margarine, became staple items. Crelos Margarine appears to be the popular Sainsbury brand; the Unilever shops sold Van den Bergh margarine. Since its American patenting in 1873, margarine had challenged butter as a reasonably cheap substitute.

Photo: Popperfoto

The draper's shop. In an age of mainly home-made dresses, curtains and so forth, the drapers' shops, with their horizontally shelved bolts of fabrics, were very necessary. The stock was very full and complete but there was little in the way of presentation or 'window dressing'. Such shops are less common today, having yielded to ready-made chain store products.

Photo: © Barnaby's Picture Library

Hayters Stores, 1920. Despite the growing dominance of chain-stores, plenty of one-man businesses pursued their specialist lines. Here poultry, rabbit, hare and game are in abundance. Few butchers now indulge in the 'home-killed' trade, and the years between the wars saw a big shift from shopkeepers preparing their own products – weighing sugar, blending tea, slaughtering rabbits – to retailing already prepared and usually branded products.

Photo: Popperfoto

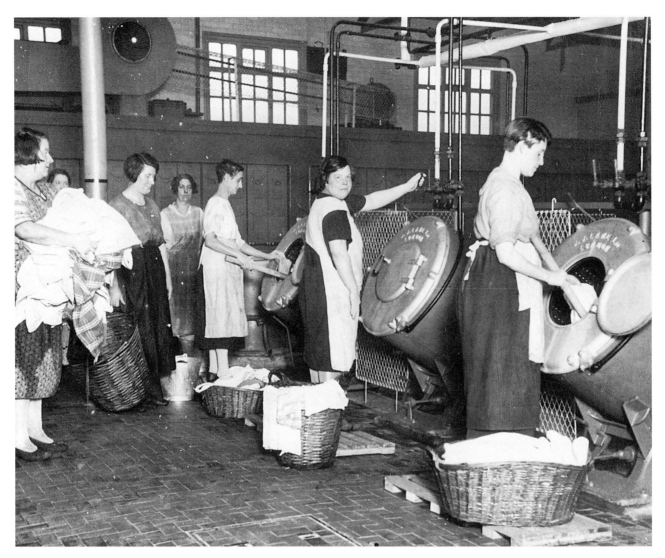

The electric rotary washing machines of Dean Lane, Moston, Manchester, 1927. This new electrified public wash-house had just been opened. It makes for a nice mid-way picture. These ladies' mothers struggled to do the wash by hand at home or manually in public wash-houses; their daughters have had an electric washing machine at home. Washing tended to be a weekly chore, with Monday usually the chosen day. Clothes are washed much more frequently now, just as people tend to have more baths and showers than in times gone by.

Photo: Documentary Photography Archive

Edinburgh's Costorphine Station, 1926. Advertising was becoming more general as consumer spending widened in character, and this bill-poster is putting up quite a show of adverts. Eating (sausages and biscuits) and drinking (beer and coffee) dominate the advertising landscape, alongside the bill for the Edinburgh Empire.

Photo: By courtesy of Edinburgh City Libraries

A 'gentleman's bar' about 1930. Eating out, either at lunch-break from work or for leisure, has been a gradually increasing activity all through this century. This typical 'gentleman's bar', suggestive of the cafeteria style, illustrates the point with some aplomb. During this time 'eating-out' spread to the lower classes, with the Lyons and ABC cafés being very popular – a well-cooked meal could be comfortably enjoyed for as little as a shilling (5p).

Photo: Popperfoto

AT SCHOOL AND WORK

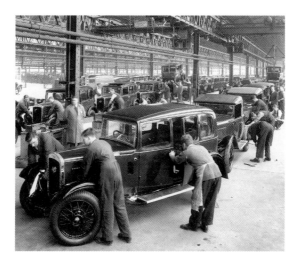

If you want to spark off the memories of older people, ask them to describe their first day at school and their first day at work. They were two very sharp culture-shocks indeed. In each case you entered a very formal and regulated structure and both the classroom and the factory were severely disciplined. You would have sat in straight lines of desks at school, and then stood at straight lines of looms or lathes at work.

There was also the sheer crowding together. For most of this period a quarter of all children were in classes of over 60 pupils and, even in 1939, a majority remained in classes of 50 or more. Those who were at school then are apt to chuckle over the anguish shown now about classes of over 30. Being crushed cheek by jowl at the pit-face or on the ship's keel, or side by side in the new-fangled typing pool, must not have seemed very different.

Gradually, cleaner, quieter and less strenuous forms of manufacture were introduced and there was a big increase in clerical work, in banking, local government and insurance. Despite the flurry of women doing men's work in the First World War, it was normally accepted that some jobs were for men and some for women.

Mechanisation was moving on apace, and it was not just the tractor on the farmer's field or the early automation of industry. In the 1920s and 1930s those two influential tools of modern life, the typewriter and the telephone, came of age. Their timing was similar. Alexander Graham Bell spoke his first telephonic sentence to his assistant, Thomas Watson, in 1876. The first typewriter had been marketed by the American gunsmiths, Remingtons, in 1874.

Gradually, they had become standard UK devices. By 1939 it was a very old-fashioned office which didn't boast both. The familiar red telephone kiosk was becoming almost as firm a favourite as the pillar box as a piece of street furniture. And it was the women who took most of the jobs on telephone switchboards and in typing pools. The old-fashioned male clerk on his high stool, scratching away at the ledger, was vanishing.

Yet there was still something of a novelty about telephones and typewriters. One woman told me that, on her first day at work, aged 14, in the 1920s, she was instructed to answer the telephone, an instrument she had never used before. Each time it rang, she paid a discreet visit to the lavatory.

The Barony Street playground, Edinburgh, around 1930.
Some efforts were made to provide play-areas for small children, especially in the towns, although if mothers were working there was much dependence on the extended family or on the neighbours. These playgrounds were a chance for toddlers to enjoy playing with tricycles and pedal cars in safety.

Photo: By courtesy of Edinburgh City Libraries

Holy Trinity School, East Finchley, 1925. Note the typically rigid rows of cramped desks and rather stiff and stern conditions. Classrooms were often grouped around a 'central hall', and the internal windows of such schools were so constructed that the seated pupils could hardly see out, but a patrolling head-teacher could see in! Survivors of that 'class' (not so much 'form' in those days) will now be in their eighties.

Photo: Mary Evans Picture Library

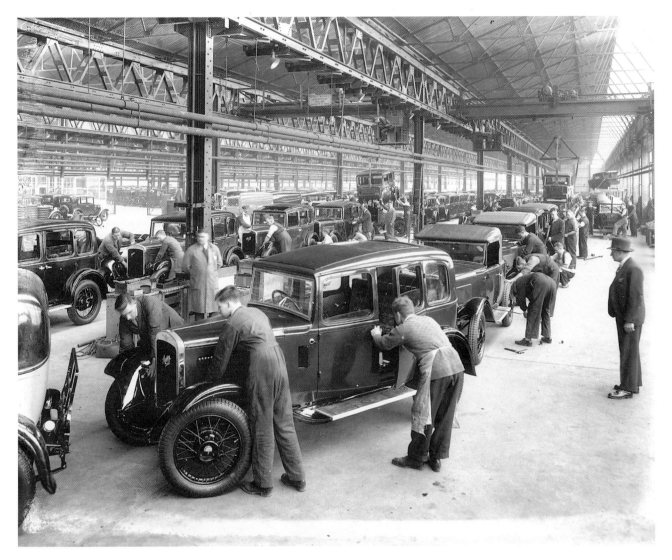

Production Line of the Austin 16hp. 6cyl. Burnham Saloon, 1930. When children left school and went to work, they might have felt quite used to the long, strictly controlled assembly lines which made up much of modern British industry. This is a good 'in between' sort of picture. Mass production has certainly replaced the old-style craftsmen at work on one item at a time, but does not yet have the smooth, automated flow of today's manufacturing.

Photo: British Motor Industry Heritage Trust/Rover Group

The Liverpool Gladstone Dock between the wars. Some industries were not yet at all modernised, and dockers still manhandled most of the goods being landed or shipped, often in poor conditions and with much insecurity of work.

Photo: Liverpool Daily Post and Echo

Colliers in the 1930s. Miners still produced coal stocks with fairly primitive equipment and in tough conditions, although, like dockers, they relied extensively on team-work and often lived close to their work-place in tight-knit communities. The miners and dockers were, predictably, among the more militant workers of the day.

Photo: © Barnaby's Picture Library

A Farm in Swabiagh, Ireland, 1926. Mechanisation was beginning to transform some aspects of farming. Tractors and other steam- or fuel-driven machinery speeded up productivity, as illustrated by this steam-powered thresher. It wasn't all that long since threshing had been done manually, but here it looks as if a work-force of six can handle it. A distinctive Ford car stands in the foreground.

Photo: © Stepney/Barnaby's Picture Library

The Wiltshire Downs, 1937. Horses still continued to play an important role on the farm. Here, while the ploughmen sit down for their lunch, the horses relax with their nose-bags. The Second World War gave the main industrial boost to farming – more land was cultivated, productivity increased, the number of horses used dropped dramatically, and mechanised horse-power on the land shot from two to five million.

Photo: Mary Evans Picture Library

Cromer Mills, Middleton, Lancashire in the 1930s. Women still found jobs as they always had done in some regions – for instance, among the noise but comparative safety of the mills and allied trades. The young women here are working in a cardroom, but a lot of other jobs done by women during World War I were now done by men again – a similar reaction would occur after World War II.

Photo: Documentary Photography Archive

The Lotus Shoe Factory, Stafford, about 1933. Increasingly, office and secretarial work was becoming a female preserve, as this typing pool shows. It looks an airy and spacious office and, despite the clatter of typewriters, the noise level would have been preferable to that of the mills. The image of the old male Dickensian clerk, sitting at a high stool, scratching away with a pen at his ledgers, had practically vanished.

Photo: Mary Evans Picture Library

Telephone girls in the 1930s. The growing practice of telephoning, for both business and domestic purposes, introduced another occupational outlet for young women on the many switchboards of the nation. Here are telephone girls helping 'callers', as they came to be known, with a supervisor in the background. Again, this picture shows how effective was this technology, but how crude and complicated it was compared with present-day electronics and computerised systems.

Photo: © Barnaby's Picture Library

IN NEED OF HELP

Needless to say, illness and other problems were never far away, so let's see how the last generation dealt with them. One thing that doesn't much change is who cares for you when there is trouble. We all know there are public services, but it is family, neighbours and friends who remain, now as then, the first port of call when social ills threaten. However, there was some piecemeal assistance even before the emergence of the full-blown Welfare State – this came after 1945 when Clement Attlee's Labour government, leaning on the Beveridge Report, consolidated and improved what had been the previous rather haphazard schemes.

These included, for example, 'panel' doctors for thousands of workers, paid for from National Insurance contributions. Then there was the spread of maternity and child welfare clinics after 1918, along with a major development of midwifery and health-visiting. Such public health provisions were beginning to pay dividends, but some scourges remained, like tuberculosis, diphtheria and rickets. The older generation will conjure up vivid images of visits to doctors, who usually ran their own dispensary, and to clinics, with maybe a steely-eyed nurse in impregnable command.

One recalls some rather odd family remedies: salt for grazes, fatty bacon on a string for sore throats, crushed eggshells for mumps, breathing in tar fumes for whooping cough. . . . But even more frightening was what the public authorities offered. There always seemed to be a massive, gaunt institution looming somewhere in the background.

If you ask some older person about this, you will probably be told about a great hospital, with towering storeys and lengthy wards; of a dread workhouse (there were still a million paupers, perhaps a fifth of them in institutions, at the outbreak of World War II); of a nearby bleak prison; of a frightening asylum – the local authorities had to cater for 100,000 'lunatics', as they were still called, during this period. These gigantic buildings stood gloomily waiting for those who, as a last resort, might be taken there.

Even so, birth and death continued, in the main, to be domesticated. As children, many of today's pensioners would have lived in a house where someone died or where a birth occurred. But even the funeral was faced with the motor car. By 1939 the question arose: is it more fashionable to take that final journey to the cemetery in a sleek limousine-type hearse or drawn by black-plumed horses?

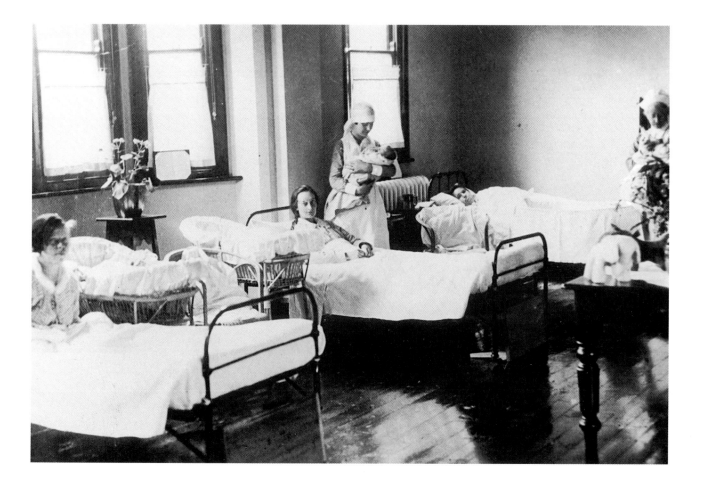

A maternity ward at Heanor, Derbyshire in the 1930s. A lot of help became more 'institutionalised' during this time, including the wider practice of hospital births. Although probably quite comfortable, the 'Nightingale'-type ward does have something of a barrack-room effect, with the highly polished floors, beds in strict military order and the severely uniformed nurse. At much the same time, the 1936 Midwives Act ensured that midwifery became a full-time, salaried service, and, in general, childbirth was very much safer than it had been.

Photo: Derbyshire Libraries and Heritage Department

A dispensary in Finchley in the 1930s. Mothers and children were increasingly cared for by local authority health visitors, clinics and dispensaries. Here we have the common sight of a well-starched nurse and the less common sight of a lady doctor, while the room itself looks a bit amateurish compared with the gleaming, sterilised, high-tech facilities of today. School medical inspection was introduced as early as 1907, and many older people have vivid memories of 'the school nurse' – her routine examination for hair 'nits' is a constant element in such reminiscence.
Photo: © Barnaby's Picture Library

The Hutchison House Home for Babies and Children, Leytonstone, in the 1930s. There were children's homes and orphanages for less fortunate youngsters, many of them organised by charitable foundations. Uniform clothing was quite usual, as this cart-load of look-alike children illustrates, and the uniformed nurses were also the norm. That whole 'institutional' flavour was to haunt this kind of well-intentioned activity for another generation.

Photo: © Barnaby's Picture Library

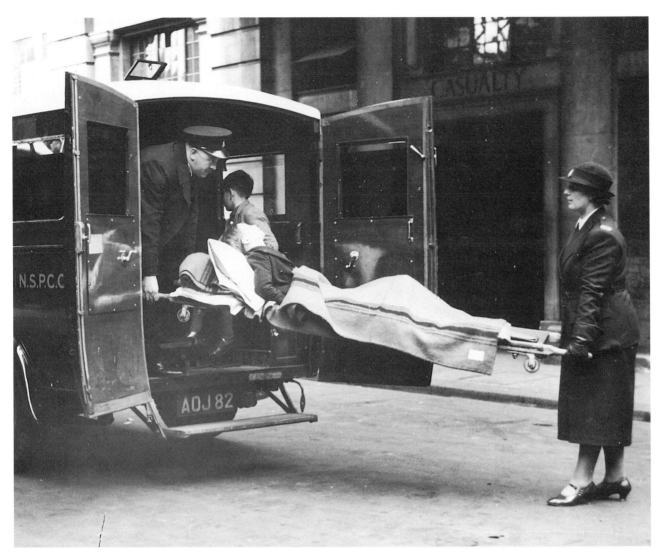

An NSPCC motorised ambulance with its sad cases at the casualty department of a large local authority hospital. This is an intriguing little cameo of voluntary body and municipal institution in partnership. Child welfare was much improved by the expanding work of health visitors, whose numbers sprang from 600 in 1910 to nearly 1,500 by 1920 and went on increasing.

Photo: © Barnaby's Picture Library

The Snow Hill Labour Exchange, Birmingham, 1930. The search for work in the depths of the depression was a heart-rending one. Most such images of that time are of flat-capped, bescarfed working men, shuffling in long, dismal queues. This picture conveys a slightly different message: there are trilbies and ties and a general air of lower middle class respectability, but, not surprisingly, the same expressions of despair and frustration.

Photo: Hulton Getty

A Liverpool policeman in 1936. The twixt-and-between world of the inter-war years is well illustrated by this policeman. He bowls ponderously along on a sit-up-and-beg bike but he is equipped with a midget wireless receiver: 'calling all cycles', if not yet the famous signal 'calling all cars'. In 1939 there were 183 police forces in England and Wales, controlled by standing committees in the counties or watch committees in boroughs of substantial size. Successive bouts of rationalisation have reduced this to 44 police forces, bringing complaints that police administration has grown a little distant from ordinary people.

Photo: Liverpool Daily Post and Echo

Pentonville Prison in about 1939. Should you have fallen foul of the law, then one of the huge, harsh gaols might have claimed you as a mailbag sewer. This is an unusual shot from inside one such large national prison, of which there were about sixty in the United Kingdom at this time. Coarsely dressed and strictly overseen, the convicts toil silently away at their boring and often painful task.

Photo: Liverpool Daily Post and Echo

A funeral in Bolton in the 1930s. Finally to the cemetery or, increasingly, the crematorium. People gather on a Bolton street to pay their last respects to a departed neighbour, carried thence in a relatively novel funeral motorcade. Such communal mourning has disappeared. For instance, on the day of the funeral the curtains would have been drawn in all the houses in the street as a mark of sorrow, and men raised their hats as a hearse passed along the road, even when the deceased was unknown to them.

Photo: Bolton Museum and Art Gallery

AT LEISURE

How did people spend their hard-earned leisure time seventy or so years ago? Thankfully, there was still time for play. Indeed, since about 1870 the time, opportunity and money for organised leisure had been growing. In spite of the harsh economic difficulties, this tendency was kept up between the two wars. Afterwards, it was onward, ever onward, to the leisure-dominated mood of the present day. Two features of the leisure pursuits of the 1919-39 era show us the shape of the ongoing change.

Firstly, recreation largely meant going out and spending money, with an increase of family jaunts and people gathering together. Thousands flocked to the variety theatres where Max Miller and his 'good companions' entertained, and the conventional theatre also remained popular. Thousands more flocked to the football grounds. Old-time soccer supporters smile when commentators now rhapsodise about big crowds. In the 1920s and '30s many grounds were packed solid with mainly standing and uncovered supporters, and there was no separation of home and visiting fans – indeed, until the motorways and better wages of the 1950s, few fans travelled away.

The dance-halls, too, attracted vast numbers, possibly reaching the peak of their popularity during the 1930s and into the '40s. These were paralleled at the other end of the social scale by the night clubs and restaurants which offered an evening of wining, dining and dancing among the rich and famous.

Yet at the same time there were signs of a retreat, especially in suburban Britain, from these more crowded scenes. There were those individual pastimes, sometimes home-based, which have grown in popularity over the last forty years. Gardening for delight, rather than just for growing vegetables, was an instance of this.

Secondly, and this is often mentioned when people reminisce about those days, there was already quite an amount of mechanised entertainment.

The prime example was the cinema, which soon began to threaten the 'live' theatre. The cinema sold 20 million tickets a week at this time, eclipsing all other commercial diversions. In regions like Scotland and Lancashire, there was one cinema seat for every nine people. Leslie Halliwell, the well-known film critic, writing of his childhood in Bolton in the 1930s, evocatively described the allure of no less than 47 cinemas within five miles of the town centre.

A pub in the 1930s. Although drunkenness was less common, the pubs still acted as one of the centres for local life. The men, hair smarmed flat, are slightly separate from the women, with hair-nets and rollers, but women are now actually in the pubs, drinking and smoking. It's a fairly humdrum establishment, far removed from the slick, refurbished hostelries of today, and there is no sign of 'pub grub'. That constant image, the child waiting at the pub door for her parents, is reflected, but to be honest, she seems happy enough, and the whole scene is a cheerful one.
Photo: © Barnaby's Picture Library

Arsenal versus Birmingham at Highbury Stadium, North London, at the beginning of the 1933-34 season. Lots of caps and hats in evidence, and there isn't a replica shirt or banner in sight. In those days, half-time scores were put up manually, using an alphabetical code by reference to the fixtures printed in your programme – the Highbury board is in the top left-hand corner. And there's just ten minutes to go to half time.

Photo: Hulton Getty

Blackheath, July 1930: a hot day for watching Kent play Surrey at cricket in the County Championship. There's a good crowd, knotted handkerchiefs are the fashion, but only one valiant spectator dares to show off his braces. Few County Championship games, as opposed to Test matches, now draw big crowds, and, when they do, the dress decorum is much more casual.

Photo: Hulton Getty

The Croydon Hippodrome about 1929 or 1930. Crowds flocked to the 'flicks' in their thousands. The Croydon Hippodrome's 'All Talking Programme' was showing '*Senor Americano*', one of the many low-budget Westerns of the era, starring ex-rodeo star, Ken Maynard. Doors opened at 1.45 p.m., probably for a 2.00 p.m. start, and one could join the programme of news, cartoons, features as well as 'big picture' at any time and then watch it round – more than once if time and inclination allowed, The catch-phrase, 'this is where I came in', comes from this practice.

Photo: BFI Films: Stills, Posters and Designs

The St James's Theatre, London, 1930, later to be demolished. This type of shot would not look unusual today, were it not for the queue. The hiring of canvas stools for queuing purposes has long been abandoned, not least because there is so much pre-booking of seats. The theatre queue idea, complete with the sale of cups of tea, was introduced from the USA into Britain by Richard D'Oyly Carte on the opening of the Savoy Theatre in 1881.

Photo: Hulton Getty

Hyde Park in 1939. Not all music was on wireless or gramophone; a stirring military or brass band on a decent summer's day could still draw a large crowd, including the nursemaid and pram. This rather smart crowd was enjoying 'Gems from the Gondoliers' or 'Selections from Souza' just two months before the outbreak of World War II, and yet it could almost be an Edwardian scene. Britain boasted something like 50,000 brass bands at this time.

Photo: © Barnaby's Picture Library

Hammersmith *Palais de Dance* in 1920. Ballroom dancing, particularly in the great dance-halls of the major towns, came into its own after the First World War and the dance-hall was, with the cinema, the prime place for courtship. There's almost a Turkish ambience, and, unlike some of the Plazas and Ritzes in the provinces, it's not overcrowded. It was to be the era of the waltz, the quickstep and the slow fox-trot, and ballroom dancing competitions were added to the entertainment.

Photo: Hulton Getty

The Café de Paris, London, September 1933. The Licensing Act of 1921 allowed drink to be served after 11.0 p.m. provided food was served, and restaurants were quick to take advantage of the dancing craze, by creating a dance-floor among the tables. With a top-class orchestra and sometimes a Noël Coward-type cabaret, London society, suitably attired in black tie or evening frock, became quite convivial. With more cars available, the 'road-house' was the middle class and provincial equivalent.

Photo: Hulton Getty

HOLIDAYS AND OUTINGS

At the beginning of the twentieth century only a minority went on holiday; at the end of the century only a minority don't. In the inter-war years about half did. By the 1930s just under seven million employees even enjoyed paid holidays.

Many holiday recollections are about their strict routine. A population trained by the austere discipline of the school bell, office clock and factory hooter was unlikely to kick over the traces too easily. Each year there were regular company and office closures and 'wakes' weeks, with school holidays arranged to fit. Families went away at the same time every year, they tended to visit the same place, and they more than likely stayed at the same boarding house, itself run by strict rules about meals, towels, bathrooms and locking-up times.

Although there was a countryside movement of hikers and cyclists, most holiday-makers went by train to the seaside resorts. The days themselves took on their own regimental design. There were walks along the proms and piers and valiant forays on to often coolish, wind-swept beaches, together with a tightly-planned routine of ice-cream, saucy postcards and donkey-rides.

Such holidays are among the brightest memories of older people. Younger people now may laugh at the sheer dullness of such mundane pleasures, but they forget one crucial point. The modern employee may have six weeks' paid holiday, plus a surplus of bank holidays. Before World War II the worker would be fortunate to have one week's holiday on full wages. It was vital not to waste it, for there was neither time nor money for a second chance. It was this that decided many to settle for what they knew. It was this that made the early holiday camps so attractive.

In 1940 the pleasure steamers were on their way to Dunkirk to rescue many of those who had enjoyed trips aboard 'the Skylark' on this side of the Channel. Possibly those virtues of organised work and recreation were to stand the British in good stead. They queued as patiently for those brave boats – just as housewives would wait in an orderly fashion for the occasional orange or packet of razor blades of wartime Britain – as they had queued for the annual holiday trains to Skegness or Bournemouth and for that annual chance to watch the Fol de Rols at the end of the pier. The time 'before the war' was over.

Westcliff, June 1919. The wholesome desire for a seaside holiday, developed during late Victorian and Edwardian times, was kept up after the First World War. Two little children enjoy a paddle against the canvas of a crowded strand. Increasingly, by train and charabanc, it became the norm to take the family for a week to the seaside.

Photo: Mary Evans Picture Library

Swanage, Dorset, in the 1930s. Another characteristic seaside scene, with mums, dads and children enjoying the adventures of Punch and Judy. They seem to have left a wide expanse of ocean to one dad and one child, with just a few boats and bathers to the left. Even the casual wear of sports jackets, frocks and pullovers appears staid compared with the fashions of the present day.

Photo: © Barnaby's Picture Library

A Tyneside charabanc outing about 1920. The charabanc, that telling symbol of the age, was like a lengthy sports car in shape. This one is full to overflowing, and the driver would not be out of place on Sunset Boulevard. This is probably a day trip to the coast or to some local beauty spot. As always in pictures of these times, the array of hats is formidable. Note the lamp and 'squeezy' horn, either side of the front of the vehicle.

Photo: © West Newcastle Local Studies/Newcastle Libraries and Information Service

91

Cromford, Derbyshire in the 1930s. Camping was the inexpensive, healthy alternative to the boarding house holiday. It was all part of the 'fresh air' movement of the times, although the tents and equipment look a trifle frail – this pair possibly need the, one hopes, hot cup of tea they have brewed.

Photo: Derbyshire Libraries and Heritage Department

A caravan holiday in the North-east in the 1930s. Another option of growing impact was the caravan holiday. This one is located on a farm, with a tent beside it to take the overflow. About this time it was also the practice to enjoy a cheap holiday in converted railway carriages, drawn into rather primitive campsites on the North Welsh coast and elsewhere.

Photo: Newcastle Libraries and Information Service

93

Derbyshire Street, Bolton, celebrate the Silver Jubilee of George V in 1935. Any excuse for a street-party became the motto in many working class areas. Two years later and the bunting and jellies would be out for the Coronation of George VI. It was a chance to bring a bit of colour to rather drab lives and was especially pleasant for children whose parents could not afford a holiday.

Photo: Documentary Photography Archive

St Moritz in 1922. At the other end of the social scale there was a hint of the foreign holidays everyone would crave from about the 1960s on. These awkwardly-skirted and knicker-bockered glories are having a skiing lesson, and there were plenty of such opportunities for the affluent minority to have a good time at mainly French and Swiss venues.

Photo: Hulton Getty

Butlin's Holiday Camp, Skegness, 1936. And so to the thrills of the new-style holiday camp. This keep-fit class at Butlin's is typical of the cheerful but strenuous and regimented regime of such holidays – and the chalets look rather like garden sheds. However, it was less sedate than most boarding house holidays and everyone had a good time. Three years later, the holiday camps would be used for war purposes and many ex-campers would be keeping fit in army and RAF camps and living in barrack-rooms.

Photo: By courtesy of Butlin's Holiday Worlds